Mills and Factories of New England

Mills and Factories of New England

Photographs by Serge Hambourg

ESSAYS BY NOEL PERRIN AND KENNETH BREISCH

CAPTIONS BY KENNETH BREISCH

HARRY N. ABRAMS, INC., PUBLISHERS, NEW YORK,

IN ASSOCIATION WITH THE

HOOD MUSEUM OF ART, DARTMOUTH COLLEGE

To Maria

S.H.

Editor: Eric Himmel
Designer: Michael Hentges

Library of Congress
Cataloging-in-Publication Data

Hambourg, Serge.
    Mills and factories of New England.

    Bibliography: p. 108
        1. Architecture, Industrial—New England—Pictorial
works—Exhibitions. 2. Factories—New England—Pictorial works—
Exhibitions. 3. Mills and mill-work–New England—Pictorial
works—Exhibitions. I. Perrin, Noel. II. Breisch, Kenneth A.
III. Hood Museum of Art. IV. Title.
TR659.H36 1988   779'.4'0924   87-25483
ISBN 0-8109-1448-4

A Times Mirror Company

Printed and bound in Japan

1 (Frontispiece). Snuff Mill and Sawmill Complex, Byfield,
Massachusetts

*Waterpower has been used to grind tobacco into snuff and mill lumber on this
site since 1804, when the first snuff mill was constructed. A second structure
was erected in 1830. Originally a sawmill, it was converted into a snuff mill
in 1860, when a new sawmill was built. In the foreground is the millpond
from which the power for these factories was derived.*

2 (These pages). Ponemah Mill, Taftville, Connecticut

*This mill, begun in 1866 and completed five years later, was the first of four
major mills constructed by the Ponemah Mill Company. The company also
built four boarding houses and over two hundred smaller dwellings for fifteen
hundred workers in the village of Taftville, named for Edward Taft, one of
the original investors in the corporation. In the late nineteenth century, the
Ponemah Mill Company was one of the most successful cotton textile
manufacturing enterprises in the country. The entire complex was designated
a National Register Historic District in 1978.*

Published on the occasion of an exhibition at the Hood Museum of
Art, Dartmouth College, Hanover, New Hampshire, March 26–
May 22, 1988, traveling to the National Building Museum,
Washington, D.C., and the Canadian Center for Architecture,
Toronto, Canada. This exhibition and catalogue have been made
possible by a grant from the Bernstein Development Foundation.

Contents

Foreword

Between 1982 and 1985, Serge Hambourg photographed over four hundred examples of historic New England industrial buildings. Hambourg's color photographs, a selection of which is presented here, achieve a fresh visual understanding of the mill, challenging the stereotypes that have controlled its popular perception. A disciplined concentration lies behind each photograph, a concentration evident, to us, as an extraordinary power of evoking presence. Indeed, "presence" here applies to both subject and object: while the buildings declare themselves in forceful images, the photographs display the formalist rigor of the artist's vision.

In this as in several other respects, Hambourg's mill series recalls Walker Evans's photographs of the homes of Alabama sharecroppers, made in 1936 and published with James Agee's text in 1941 as *Let Us Now Praise Famous Men*. Agee was moved by the stark eloquence he and Evans discovered in the weathered clapboard surfaces—"their tensions sprung against centers and opposals of . . . rigid and earned exactitude." Twenty years later, in an April 1956 portfolio of color photographs in *Fortune* magazine, Evans discovered similar virtues in the mill architecture of the eastern United States. Those "thousands of time-brushed buildings," Evans wrote, "make a relatively cheerful if incomplete answer to the foreboding question asked by William Blake as the Industrial Revolution darkened England's green and pleasant land: 'And was Jerusalem builded here/Among these dark Satanic Mills?'"

Hambourg's work suggests a similar affirmation. Here too, vernacular structures answer so well to the photographer's quest for form that the breakings and balancings of pattern seem "composed" in a musical sense. Hambourg is particularly responsive to the elongations characteristic of the building type. Major horizontals appear to travel across the visual plane, impelled by a lyrical momentum. Often the building simply continues out of the visual frame, like a passing train. Sometimes the movement is completed like a musical phrase: the cornice of a brick facade makes a flourish and coda at the building's turn, or a curving dock extends the presence of a tiny building, note by note, into the midst of a vast water. Passionately contemplative, relishing elisions between subject and form, Hambourg, like Evans, draws upon both Romantic and Modernist aesthetic legacies in representing vernacular architecture.

In the essays that follow, Noel Perrin and Kenneth Breisch address the complex issues raised by these photographs. As Perrin points out, the Romantic anti-industrial homiletic is challenged by New England's rural experience of the mill as "a symbiosis between the pastoral and the mechan-

3. Little River Mill, East Lebanon, Maine

This waterpowered gristmill and shingle mill was built of hand-hewn timbers in 1774 by Joseph Hardison. A millstone used to grind the grain from neighboring farms can be seen in the foreground. Small industrial buildings like this one are precursors of the first textile mills.

ical." Breisch, on the other hand, emphasizes the central role of the mill in the process of urbanization. Hambourg explores the full range of this complex iconic history. There are picturesque evocations of the mill's pastoral legacy, as well as images of the numbing loneliness of large urban structures in abandoned areas. The dominant note, however, is that of the "mixed landscape," as Perrin calls it, thick with traces of both rural and industrial contexts.

The mill was already a well-worn poetic theme by 1860, when George Eliot drew upon its conflicting associations for *The Mill on the Floss:* the landscape, which stimulates a childlike nostalgia for pastoral tranquility, versus the river, the flux of time, change, and experience. Hambourg savors the accumulation of resonances about his subject, just as he enjoys the interplay of forms and surfaces. Symbolically, the mill figures as an interface between field and city, as well as between agrarian and industrial eras of American history. It embodies the human invasion of nature that became a "second nature"—first through the dependence upon natural resources, then as ruin.

Fifteen years ago, an exhibition on the subject of New England mill architecture would have suggested a fairly predictable lesson. The building type would have summoned forth the design principle that form follows function, illustrating the link between vernacular architecture and modernism. Anticipations of functionalist thinking in New England culture would have been cited, like Horatio Greenough's attack on "embellishment" as "false beauty." Keenly aware of this line of thinking, architectural historian Kenneth Breisch provides us with a useful account of the technical achievements that attracted modernist scholars like Sigfried Giedion to mill structures. However, Breisch also places the mill within the social history of industrialism, linking it to rapid technological change, social displacement, and urban growth. The architectural development of the mill can thus be seen as marking the transition from the stability of the rural village to the stresses of the industrial city, which served more as a "place of encampment" for immigrant workers than a lifelong residence.

Noel Perrin also emphasizes the mill's role in a changing New England, but focuses on the environmental and aesthetic complexities of the "mixed landscape" produced by industrial transformation. Writing from the locally grounded perspective that his essays have made famous (*First Person Rural* and his two subsequent collections), Perrin challenges the conventional antitheses between nature and culture, farming and industry. Thetford, Vermont, provides the new/old archeological text: the fields too are manufactured, and yesterday's defaced landscape has become today's picturesque ruin. In this sense, the crucial fact about the mill is its ultimate adaptability. Reuse in its profoundest sense—as the affirmation of change—becomes the new meaning of the mill by the river, displacing our nostalgia for the pastoral myth.

Some will call this a "regional" project, with condescending intent. The commentaries of Breisch and Perrin, which explore a range of architectural, social, and ecological issues pertinent to these photographs, amply demonstrate their general significance. Moreover, the aesthetic distinction of Serge Hambourg's work constitutes another, equally eloquent order of significance. There is no need, however, to apologize for the "local." Locally generated virtues such as craftsmanship, economy, technical ingenuity, and responsiveness to context have informed this building type through all its mutations, and not the least of Mr. Hambourg's achievements was finding ways to make these virtues visually comprehensible. Many of our best writers have called attention to the importance of regional perspectives, from Henry Thoreau and William Carlos Williams to contemporaries like Donald Hall, Edward Hoagland, and (indeed) Noel Perrin. The basic lesson, however, has required constant restating—that the pragmatic concreteness and unselfconscious vitality of local expression constitute the distinctive message of American culture. The photographs and essays in this book remind us of this in important ways. In the process they contribute to a distinguished legacy of vision and interpretation.

This photographic project, conceived by Serge Hambourg, was supported by the Canadian Center for Architecture. We would like to express our appreciation to Phyllis Lambert and Richard Pare of the CCA. The staff of the Hood Museum of Art also deserves thanks. Assistant director Timothy F. Rub, registrar Rebecca A. Buck, exhibition curators Evelyn Marcus and Robert Raiselis, assistants Hilary Ragle and Susan Moody, all contributed in special ways to the success of this enterprise. Eric Himmel, an editor at Harry N. Abrams, Inc., was an essential member of our team. The final form of this publication owes a great deal to his intelligent and critical suggestions at every stage of the project. We would also like to acknowledge the contribution of designer Michael Hentges. Finally, I would like to extend warmest thanks to Raphael Bernstein, who first introduced me to Serge Hambourg and his work, and who has been an indispensable advisor and supporter in this as in so many other projects at the Hood Museum of Art.

JACQUELYNN BAAS
Director
Hood Museum of Art, Dartmouth College

A Mixed Landscape

Noel Perrin

In the northwestern corner of Connecticut, there is a pretty little town called Colebrook. The landscape is serene and pastoral. The two main villages, Colebrook Center and North Colebrook, have both recently become National Historic Districts.

About fifty years ago, a small boy spent many summer days exploring the woods of North Colebrook, near his uncle's farm. One afternoon he happened on a many-windowed old building, deep in the woods. (At least that was how it struck his nine-year-old mind. Actually the building stood less than fifty feet from an old town road.) It didn't feel like an abandoned house. Looking back, he would remember the absence of lilacs in the dooryard, and the fact that no one side seemed to be clearly the front.

But that day he spent little time trying to figure out what the structure must have been. He was too interested in the gleam of the afternoon sun on the old small-paned windows. Many panes, of course, were broken. But even more were not—it was as if they had been saved specially for him. Without making anything that could be called a conscious decision, he looked among the roots of the birches and pines for a stone of suitable size. New England soil being what it is, he quickly found one. He threw it. With a fine splintering crash, a pane of glass broke.

This was too keen a pleasure not to repeat, and he went to look for another rock. He threw again, and another pane went tinkling in. Soon he shifted to a better source of missiles: a pile of rosy old bricks, mostly fragmented, that he found on the north side of the building. Pieces of brick throw well. Before he started back to his uncle's house, he had broken every remaining pane on the first floor, and most on the second. When he got home to supper, he said nothing about the adventure to his aunt and uncle. Experience had taught him that anything that much fun was likely to be disapproved of by adults.

Years later, when he was a relatively sophisticated college student, he dated a girl in Colebrook Center whose mother was trying to assemble enough panes of wavy old glass to reglaze all the windows of a Colonial house she was restoring. Listening to the mother, he felt almost awed by how much history he had been able to smash in a single afternoon. By then he also knew what history it was. He knew that the building he had found was the old cheese factory in North Colebrook—one of the thousands of industrial ruins that were and still are scattered across New England. The mother's passion affected him. If given a chance, he would retroactively have saved those windows.

4. Mill, New Preston, Connecticut

This mill is one of almost a dozen small industrial operations that drew their power from the small creek flowing out of Lake Waramaug and through the center of New Preston. In the foreground, raised on a stone foundation, can be seen the wheelhouse, which still encloses an intact mill wheel.

But another dozen years had to pass before he began to think in terms of beauty as well as of history. Now a teacher, husband, and father, he had come to own an old house himself: an 1820 Federal brick farmhouse in eastern Vermont. He and his wife had bought it cheap because the roof had been about to fall in.

The front and both ends of the house had been modernized sometime around 1900. Among other things, the original windows had been replaced with Victorian two-over-twos—easy to clean and quite homely. But whoever did the job had economized on the back. There the original small-paned windows remained: nine-over-sixes, wavy glass with an occasional tiny air bubble. Each pane was different. Those windows took a lot of scraping and puttying, and before he had finished, the grown man had fallen in love with old window glass. It now struck him that he might have destroyed more beauty by throwing bricks at the cheese factory than he would have by, say, chopping down the apple trees in his uncle's orchard. Apple trees grow again.

In no way do I blame myself for taking more than twenty years to come to see beauty in the North Colebrook cheese factory. Windows apart, it can never have been a specially handsome building. Anyway, it was a *factory,* set down in a pastoral landscape, and I was raised in the tradition of the Romantic poets. In this tradition, nature is a healing force and industry is a disease, a kind of blight. Industry attacks a green valley the way mycelium attacks a green leaf. In extreme cases it will leave the valley black.

The opposition can be put in religious terms as well as medical, and it often was. The most famous single reference to industry in the poetry of the Romantics was made by William Blake. And what did he say? He said that "dark Satanic Mills" were taking over England's green and pleasant land. God is a shepherd, as we know from the 23rd Psalm. The devil turns out to be an engineer.

The thought is one that precedes the Romantics. Milton had it, for example. In his story, God designed that green and pleasant place, the Garden of Eden. Satan meanwhile set up smelting plants in hell, and went into the business of producing iron, copper, and tin. He also built the first firearms plant. Samuel Colt's factory in Hartford, Connecticut, came much later.

The thought is still with us now. You find it, for example, in Tolkien's *Lord of the Rings,* where Saruman's fortress-factory of Isengard is a type of hell, and Saruman himself a satanic figure, master of many furnaces. Isengard (the name seems to mean Iron Shield) is eventually conquered and redeemed by an assault of the trees, by ents and huorns, much as the North Colebrook cheese factory was surrounded and finally conquered by birches and pines.

Milton, Blake, and Tolkien were not wholly wrong, either. Factories and mines do frequently blight landscapes. There is a blighted landscape not three miles from where I live—a vast ruined

5. Manomet Mill, New Bedford, Massachusetts

The late date of the Manomet Mill, which was erected in 1903, is betrayed by the large scale of the window openings that have now been filled with fiberglass panels. These are set between brick piers and spanned by segmental brick arches and granite lintels. This mill, which is now owned by the Cliftex Corporation, is still being used to produce textiles and clothing.

slope covered with tailings from the Strafford copper mine. The mine closed in 1954; the slope stays poisoned. It will be so for many decades to come.

But not all mills are satanic, and I think especially few of them may be in New England, where from the very beginning there has been a symbiosis between the pastoral and the mechanical. That is, we have always had what I think is called a mixed economy. The early farmers produced and marketed handmade nails in their spare time: They were metal-workers as well as shepherds of flocks. The early mill owners were apt to keep (and sometimes personally milk) a family cow, just as an early philosopher like Emerson raised (and sometimes personally fed) an annual pig.

The result is that we have always had what could be called a mixed landscape. Fields and forests and factories have co-existed—not always happily, but often. And it is worth remembering that though the forests were here before the first Indian, let alone the first white person, set foot in what is now New England, and hence can be called natural, the fields and the factories are both man-made. One is undoubtedly more artificial than the other, but both are, in the literal sense of the word, manufactured, since the "facture" part means *to make,* and the "manu" part means *hand.* Handmade fields and handmade factories in early New England. Both are apt to have stone walls.

The mixed landscape of my own town in Vermont makes a good example. Thetford has historically been farming country—better farmland than Colebrook, because fewer rocks. Even now, when the almost-insane policies of the United States Department of Agriculture, reinforced by the universal determination of teenagers to be consistent and wash down their junk food with junk beverages, are rapidly destroying dairy farms, even now Thetford farmers ship much milk. That means many cows in town. And that in turn means many beautiful pastures, because cows are wonderful keepers of fields. They can produce greensward on which the grass is so neatly cropped that the suburban lawn was developed in conscious imitation. They can clip around rocks and up to walls far more deftly than any human with a string trimmer. They will keep all trees (except evergreens) pruned up to a uniform height—namely the five feet which is a cow's convenient reach when she has her head raised and her tongue out at comfortable leaf-flicking distance. As I write, the twenty-six acres of pasture on my own farm are in just such condition, kept so by the seventeen Jerseys and Herefords and young Holsteins who spent the summer here.

But the seal of the town of Thetford, which is rather elaborate, shows a tree-bordered lake, a good-sized factory beside a river, and a dairy farm with twin silos poking up above the barn. Underneath are three legends: Scenic Beauty—Industry—Agriculture.

Go a hundred feet east from the easternmost edge of my farm, and you will come to that river. You will not see any factories. The one on the seal exists, and still operates, but it's four miles upstream, on the far edge of town. What you will see is the covered bridge that takes our road, once called Mill Street, into the village of Thetford Center. Just below that you will see a partly ruined dam, and below that the Ompompanoosuc River cascading down a long series of rapids. The dam is concrete and fairly modern. A local farmer named Charles Vaughan built it in 1916, and brought electricity to the village.

Keep looking. There are many birch trees and young elms (this is a beautiful place), and in the summer not all the old foundations are easy to spot. But they're there. Look over at the far bank of the little river, and you will gradually notice one massive stone foundation after another. A hundred and thirty years ago there were five mills in a row along the river here, and there were three dams, one below the other, to supply them with waterpower. Thetford Center was a mill village, but it was neither dark nor satanic.

Industry came to the village around 1806, when a couple of local men set up a carding and cloth-dressing mill. Over the next half-century, more different kinds of factories lined up their waterwheels next to it than you might think possible. A carriage factory sprang up, and a factory that made window sashes and shutters. (You can still see shutters of its distinctive design all over town.) Also a potato-starch factory, a scythe and ax factory (with a one-person work force), a musical instrument factory, an axle-tree maker, a cabinet shop. A piece of furniture made there is now in the Metropolitan Museum in New York.

Most of these "factories" were tiny—if they *had* been satanic, they would have been run by imps, not full-grown devils—and most of them lasted only for ten or fifteen years. Then the building and the wheel and the water rights would pass to someone else.

But wars, which invariably produce war profiteers, are a great stimulus to industry. During the Civil War, and for a decade or two after it, little Thetford Center came to have several large manufacturing plants. Well, middle-sized, anyway. One, called the Noosuc Mill, was half a mile downriver from the covered bridge. It employed about twenty-five people, and it made a thick, tough, yellowish paper known as strawboard and also the binder's board used for hardcover books. A few years ago, when my wife had our kitchen remodeled, there turned out to be a double layer of that heavy yellow paper under the kitchen floor as insulation. Not too surprising, I suppose, because our house was once owned by Horace Brown, a native of Thetford Center who fought in the Civil War as an army captain. His first move when he came home was to buy the Noosuc Mill, and he ran it until he started a shoe factory, still further downstream. One would expect him to insulate his own house with his own strawboard. What you might not expect is that this small-time industrial magnate would have a large barn built onto the end of his house, complete with inside silo for storing winter cattle feed. But he did.

Finally, nearly a mile below the bridge, was the woolen mill, which ran from late in the Civil War until about 1880, and which in its best days had about fifty employees. It must have been a stunning sight to see all those mills running at once, all those waterwheels turning, and the great

6–8. Brooks Hardware Factory, Chester,
Connecticut

*Simon Brooks, who founded the Brooks Hardware
Company in 1848 to produce screw eyes, erected his
first factory building on this site in 1857. A second
building was constructed in 1886 and the office and
packing room followed in 1902. In 1928, the company
was incorporated as M. S. Brooks and Sons, and,
although recently sold, it still produces Simon Brooks
original product, which can be seen on the sorting
tables (plate 7). Each worker made his own work stool
(plates 7 and 8).*

leather belts taking the power from the wheelshafts to the machinery. The falls may have been more beautiful then than they are now, when there are only the half-broken dam and the half-hidden foundations of some of the mills to frame the view.

Even the great villainous industry of this part of Vermont has left beauty behind it. Some six or seven miles from Captain Brown's house is another and much older copper mine than the one in Strafford. This one had its beginning back in 1820, when people living along Copperfield Brook in the town of Vershire organized what was called the Farmers' Company. The farmers dug a little ore by hand. They also "erected a rude smelting furnace," as a man named Hamilton Child put it in 1888. They even made a little money.

But they had neither the capital nor the technology to do large-scale mining. Serious operations didn't begin until six New York City investors bought the mineral rights in 1853 and set up business as the Vermont Copper Mining Company. They put in some serious furnaces, and by the end of the Civil War around a hundred and fifty people were working at the mine and the adjacent smelter. Then, just about the time Captain Brown came home from the Civil War to take over the strawboard plant, a still richer investor from New Jersey named Smith Ely took over what soon became known as the Ely Mine. (And the little village of Copperfield became the growing new village of Ely.) Where there had been three farmhouses in 1850, there were now a hundred families living, plus two churches and a dance hall.

Smith Ely thought big. The miners, all four hundred of them, worked by candlelight—one candle per miner. But the smelting plant went modern. By the late 1870s he had a refinery seven hundred feet long and sixty-two feet wide. He had twenty-four furnaces and seventy desulphurizing ovens. He was making copper 95 percent pure, where the early farmers thought they had done well to get the proportion of copper up to 12 or 14 percent before they shipped their product off to more sophisticated refineries on the coast.

Smith Ely had also produced a miniature version of contemporary acid rain. Twenty-four furnaces make a lot of smoke. Smoke of this kind contains a lot of sulphur dioxide. His first achievement was to produce a defoliation of the hillsides along Copperfield Brook as thorough and as devastating as that which later Americans produced in Vietnam. Next to go was farming up and down the valley, as the grass died. About then a new kind of Farmers' Company formed, and, since there was no Environmental Protection Agency to complain to, the farmers complained directly to the mine officials. They may even have waved pitchforks in a menacing fashion. And the officers of the Vermont Copper Mining Company responded just exactly as the EPA would have made them a century later. They figured out a way to spread the pollution around, so that people in the valley would get a lot less and everyone for miles around would get a little bit more.

The technology didn't exist then to put up the kind of EPA-mandated giant smokestack that now distributes industrial pollution so freely across the United States and even around the world—but Vermont is hilly country, and an early version of pollution-sharing *was* possible. The Vermont Copper Mining Company dug a six-foot-deep trench all the way up the side of a small mountain behind the smelting works. Today you'd probably put a non-corroding pipeline up such a trench. They didn't have the technology for that, either. Instead, with men and oxen they brought stones and they made the trench into a walled tunnel. It rises five hundred feet, from where the smelter used to be to the top of the hill, and it is nearly half a mile long. All that way they capped it with huge flat rocks—rocks as big as double beds, some of them, and four to six inches thick. These were fitted so tightly as to be smoke-proof. The smoke was forced up to the summit, where it caught the wind and rode out across eastern Vermont, to begin its descent into other valleys.

Partly because there was never a railroad up to Copperfield, so that the coal had to come in nine miles on wagons and the copper had to leave the same way, the Ely Mine failed in the 1880s. Easier mines to work were being discovered, first in Michigan and then still further west. But there is no ghost town, as there might be in Colorado. Dry climates preserve abandoned industrial sites indefinitely; tropical jungles swallow them up almost at once. Vermont is somewhere in between.

Today there are no traces of the seven-hundred-foot smelting plant (or the dance hall, either), except on a few acres of level ground so poisoned that trees still can't grow. There you can sometimes pick up a fragment of an imported Scottish fire brick, packed into the silty yellow rubble. Just above that spot, however, and across the brook, the once-desolate hillsides are handsome with oak and birch. Isengard is fallen.

But not entirely, not yet. The stone tunnel up the hillside is still there, now lost in trees. It is one of the most beautiful ruins I know. Some of the capstones have fallen in, and a few at the lower end are missing, presumably hauled away by people who know a beautiful slab when they see one. Where the tunnel is thus uncovered, sometimes a young tree is growing right inside it. At these roofless spots you can see the inner stonework on the two sides of the tunnel. It is better drystone wall than I can build, though I have been repairing old walls and building new ones on Captain Brown's farm for twenty years.

When I first saw that solemn ruin in the woods, I had no idea what its function had been. None of the select few people I have taken to see it have guessed, either. They have imagined miners running down it in the winter, with wheelbarrow loads of ore. They have imagined water rushing down a sluice—though once we reach the top of the little mountain, and there is no brook up there where the tunnel ends, or so much as a wet spot, they've had to give *that* theory up. In the end, they've had to be told, as I was.

But not one has failed to be impressed, as one might be by a pyramid. The final legacy of Copperfield Village has been an addition to the natural beauty of the region, a human accent mark on the hill.

Industry comes and goes in New England. Right now more is coming than going, at least in the part where I live. At this very minute there is a proposal to rebuild the dam below the covered bridge in Thetford Center and resume the generation of electricity. There is also resistance to the proposal, both because a lot of trees would be cut down and a homely little powerhouse built, and because a historic site would be disturbed. (The irony, of course, is that it's historic for waterwheels and other forms of power generation.)

I see no assurance that present or future waves of factory building will leave such handsome remains behind as former ones have. One or two of the pictures in this book show modern factories that strike me as stunningly ugly. If I imagine a boy giant throwing stones at them until they are smashed, I see a ruin of concrete and plastic that would simply be a blight on our green and pleasant land. But it is notoriously hard to judge one's own time. I have seen pictures of Copperfield Village in its heyday and it was an ugly sight, too. If I had lived then, I think I would have said that that corner of Vershire was ruined, probably forever. I think I would not have imagined people coming a century later to stare in awe at the smelter chimney.

It may be that unless we manage to kill off trees altogether (in which case we'll presumably kill ourselves off, too), it may be that the alternating cycles of farm and factory will keep making the New England landscape richer and richer. At least it would be nice to think so.

9. Collins Ax Company, Collinsville, Connecticut

In 1826, Samuel and David Collins converted their gristmill and sawmill into America's first mechanized ax factory. By the 1860s, they were producing fifteen hundred axes a day, as well as machetes and other types of cutting tools, in a factory complex that eventually covered some eighteen acres of land on the banks of the Farmington River. Around this complex they developed the town of Collinsville to house the families that worked in their plant. To the left, in this view, can be seen the mill dam, which insured a steady supply of power to the Collins factory.

New England Mills

Kenneth Breisch

The Town is Galloway. The Merrimack River, broad and placid, flows down to it from the New Hampshire hills, broken at the falls to make a frothy havoc on the rocks, foaming on over ancient stone towards a place where the river suddenly swings about in a wide and peaceful basin, moving on now around the flank of the town, on to places known as Lawrence and Haverhill, through a wooded valley, and on to the sea at Plum Island, where the river enters an infinity of waters and is gone. Somewhere far north of Galloway, in headwaters close to Canada, the river is continually fed and made to brim out of endless sources and unfathomable springs. . . .

The textile factories built of brick, primly towered, solid, are ranged along the river and the canals, and all night the industries hum and shuttle. This is Galloway, milltown in the middle of fields and forests.

Jack Kerouac, *The Town and the City*, 1950

With the exception of a handful of mercantile centers, the landscape of America at the time of the Revolution was largely agricultural. In New England it comprised a scattering of small villages set amidst pastures and fields carved out of the ubiquitous forest. Here and there a gristmill or sawmill clung to the embankment of a stream or river, a lone windmill crowned a hill, or a lime kiln belched acrid smoke into the otherwise pristine air. These were local, family-owned industries, existing solely to service an agricultural economy: grinding its grain, forging its tools, and milling its lumber. So it was as one traveled southward to Spanish Florida—save that cotton or tobacco plantations replaced the villages—or west towards the wilderness beyond the Appalachians.[1] Isolated survivors of this arcadian industrial past can be found throughout New England in places such as East Lebanon, Maine, Byfield, Massachusetts, or Hampton, New Hampshire (plates 1, 3, 4, 10, and 40–44).

Almost before the new American government was formed, however, the seeds of profound change were being sown on the banks of the Blackstone River in Pawtucket, Rhode Island. Here, in 1790, was established the country's first successful, mechanized cotton-spinning manufactory in an old mill. With its abundance of rivers, surplus of capital, and ready source of labor, New England provided an almost perfect location for the new textile industry. Its cool, damp climate proved ideal for the processing into thread—and then cloth—of cotton, a plant whose natural fibers become stronger when exposed to humidity. As a consequence, between 1790 and 1850, New

10. Richmond Furnace, Richmond, Massachusetts

This kiln originally formed a part of the Richmond Ironworks, active between 1830 and 1923. The great hollow furnace was filled with a mixture of iron ore, lime, and charcoal, which was baked at a high temperature with bellows that forced air through the arched openings in its base. The lime acted as a flux to draw impurities ("dross") from the ore upward to the top of the kiln, where it was skimmed away, leaving relatively pure iron behind.

England industrialists opened or rebuilt some fourteen hundred factories devoted to the spinning and weaving of cotton alone.[2] By mid-century then, the cotton mill was firmly established as a new industrial form in the New England countryside.

Gathered around these individual mills or factory complexes came new villages and towns erected to house their employees. The buildings that composed this industrial landscape—the mills themselves, the small workers' cottages and boarding houses—as well as the dams, millponds, and canals that formed the source of power for this industry were ultimately products of the utilitarian demands of unbridled capitalist enterprise. Their basic forms evolved slowly and empirically over the first half of the century, the result of a pragmatic collaboration between factory owners and local builders and contractors. The majority of these structures thus share a common vocabulary of forms and elements that fall into the vernacular building tradition; a tradition fundamentally unaffected by the vicissitudes of architectural fashion.

The versatile design of the textile mill was soon adapted by other industries in the nineteenth century: brass factories in Connecticut, paper mills in western Massachusetts and Maine, and machine works in Providence. Around them, too, were erected similar villages of cottages and tenements to house their workers. Many of these durable buildings survive to the present-day. After decades of neglect, they have proved themselves to be ideal for reuse as spaces for everything from condominiums and malls to the manufacture of microchips. Like the buildings that line the river in Jack Kerouac's imaginary milltown of Galloway, the New England factory and its village have become an integral and living part of the common language of the American landscape.

The Evolution of the Factory

Modern textile manufacturing began in England in the 1760s as a result of technical improvements in weaving and spinning. In 1769 Richard Arkwright patented a "water-frame" capable of turning unspun cotton into yarn using a mechanical system that incorporated multiple spindles.[3] Because it required a significant source of power, Arkwright's spinning frame had to be removed from the cottage—where cotton thread had traditionally been produced by hand on small wooden spinning wheels—to a larger building and powered by either a horse gin or waterwheel. In 1769, in Nottingham, Arkwright erected such a structure to house his spinning frames, which he powered with six horses harnessed to a horizontal wheel. Two years later, in partnership with Samuel Need and Jedediah Strutt, he erected a second mill building at Cromford on the Derwent River in Derby and within a year was employing some six hundred people in this manufacturing enterprise. Here, however, his cotton-spinning machinery was powered by water.

11. Old Slater Mill, Pawtucket, Rhode Island

The Old Slater Mill, begun in 1793, was the first factory in the United States to be conceived from the beginning as a textile mill. The original building, which was expanded in the early nineteenth century, seems to have been two stories in height and approximately fifty feet long by thirty feet wide. It had a heavy timber frame covered with wooden siding laid vertically. The trapdoor or eyebrow monitor—the row of windows set into the roof to light the attic of the building—was probably added during one of the early-nineteenth-century remodelings. It, along with the small cupola or belfry that originally crowned the gable end of the mill, was to become a standard feature in early American textile factory design.

12 and 13. The Wilkinson Mill and Sylvanus
Brown House, Pawtucket, Rhode Island

*The Wilkinson Mill, erected next to the Old Slater
Mill by Oziel Wilkinson and his sons in 1810, still
houses an assortment of waterpowered machines typical of those used during the middle of the nineteenth
century. Both the roof with its trapdoor monitor and
the cupola have recently been restored to their nineteenth-century appearance. The Sylvanus Brown
House, in the left foreground of plate 12, was built in
1758. Brown was a millwright and machinist employed by many Pawtucket Valley mill owners, including Samuel Slater, to construct textile machinery and
mill dams. After his death, this home served as a
boarding house for local mill workers.*

14 and 15. Marcy Mill, Hillsboro, New Hampshire

In 1828, Joshua Marcy erected a mill building to produce cotton yarn, wadding, and batting. With its gable-end stair tower (detail in plate 14) and clerestory dormer, it—like the very similar Cheshire Mill No. 1 in nearby Harrisville (plate 56)—represents an excellent example of a typical, mid-sized, early-nineteenth-century New England textile mill. In the background is the Contoocook Mill (plate 46).

Under this system, which was more economical than either horses or steam, the spinning frames were linked by pulleys and leather belts, rotating wooden shafts and gears, to a wooden wheel, which was driven by a constant flow of water that was diverted to it from the river by means of a canal or headrace. This wheel was turned by the weight of the water, which flowed down a sluice into wooden buckets that were arrayed along its outer rim. As the wheel rotated, the water spilled out of these buckets at its base into a wheelpit and then was directed through a lower canal, or tailrace, back into the river. In order to obtain sufficient power to accomplish this, it was necessary to locate waterpowered factories just below a point where a significant drop (usually ten to fifteen feet) in the level of a stream or river naturally occurred, or to construct a dam above the headrace. The latter option, by impounding excess water in a pond that formed behind the dam, helped insure a constant supply of water, and thus power, all year around. Millponds and races, as well as constantly rotating waterwheels, thus became common features of the waterpowered factory complex in both Britain and America.

Numerous other factories modeled on the Arkwright system and licensed under his patent were soon constructed along the rivers of England and Scotland. Though most cloth continued to be woven by hand using the thread produced in the factories, the combined output from the spinning mills radically increased the overall production of cotton textiles in Britain, which monopolized world textile production by severely restricting the export of textile manufacturing machinery and any information related to its design or construction.

When the young man named Samuel Slater left England for America in 1789, however, he brought his knowledge of this industry with him, for he had begun work at age fourteen for Arkwright's partner, Jedediah Strutt, in 1776. During the ensuing years, he had not only designed and constructed textile machinery but he had also supervised the erection of at least one mill building. Consequently, by 1790, Slater, in partnership with Moses Brown and William Almy of Providence, was able to reproduce the Arkwright system in a small, remodeled mill building on the Blackstone River in Pawtucket. Three years later, these same men completed construction of the first factory building in the United States that was designed specifically to house spinning machinery. This structure now forms part of the Old Slater Mill Complex that still stands in Pawtucket (plate 11).[4]

The form of Slater's original mill seems to have been determined by its function, which required well-lighted and open work spaces capable of accommodating multiple spinning frames. Though somewhat smaller than contemporary British textile mills, the underlying concept for this factory, like the machinery it was designed to house, was based upon Slater's earlier English experience. In Pawtucket he erected a building two-and-a-half stories high and approximately fifty

16. Phoenix Iron Foundry Machine Shop, Providence, Rhode Island

The machine shop, seen on the right in this photograph, is the oldest surviving structure of the Phoenix Iron Foundry, organized by George D. Holmes in 1830 to manufacture machinery used for dying, bleaching, and printing of textile fabrics. Constructed in 1848, the stone building has a trapdoor monitor window to light the attic.

17. Busiel-Seeburg Mill, Laconia, New Hampshire

This brick hosiery factory, the eastern half of which was built by the J. W. Busiel Company in 1853, has recently been restored and adapted for use as professional office space. The stair tower and western half of the building were added in the 1870s. The attic is lighted with hip-roofed dormer windows.

18. Monadnock Mills Company, Mill No. 2, Claremont, New Hampshire

The Sugar River Manufacturing Company, which was the forerunner of the Monadnock Mills Company, was formed by a group of local entrepreneurs in Claremont and chartered in 1831. Mill No. 1, which still stands along the banks of the Sugar River, was erected by these investors between 1836 and 1845. In 1853, this second factory was constructed by what was by then the Monadnock Mills Company. Its four-story facade is marked by a prominently machicolated stair tower.

19. Comstock, Cheney and Company, Ivoryton, Connecticut

This three-story brick factory was erected in 1905 and the clock tower added about a decade later. It produced piano actions that were assembled with ivory piano keys, which Comstock, Cheney and Company had begun producing in 1849 and from which the town of Ivoryton takes its name. In the 1930s, Comstock, Cheney and Company merged with Pratt, Read and Company.

20. Dexter Richards and Sons Mill, Newport, New Hampshire

Erected about 1905, the Dexter Richards and Sons Mill stands on the site of the earlier Sugar River Mill, established in 1847 to produce cotton and wool twilled fabrics. Its thin, vertical pilasters and large window openings are indicative of its late construction date. The owners still found it necessary, however, to mark their enterprise with a traditional stair tower, in a Medieval Lombard style with a triple arcade and flaring hipped roof to crown it.

21–23. Salmon Falls Manufacturing Company, Rollinsford, New Hampshire

The Salmon Falls Manufacturing Company was established in 1822 by local New Hampshire investors and sold to the Boston firm of Mason and Lawrence in 1843, under whose guidance the town and mills grew to their present size. The weather vane (plate 22) that crowns the six-level Tuscan stair tower attached to Mill No. 1 is an emblem of the company. The mill in plate 21 with its prominent white clerestory was constructed in 1865. During its most prosperous years in the nineteenth century, the company employed some six hundred persons, who produced almost nine million yards of cotton cloth a year. Like many other New England textile enterprises, it closed its doors in 1927.

In addition to the mills themselves, numerous brick double houses and tenements, as well as the grander residence of the company agent, were all constructed by the Salmon Falls Manufacturing Company. The latter (plate 23), with its fashionable Second Empire Mansard roof, was erected in 1867. The company agent was charged with overseeing the operation of the mills for the nonresident investors, and so it was only appropriate that his house should overlook the much more modest homes of the mill's operatives.

24 and 25. Pontoosuc Woolen Mill, Pittsfield, Massachusetts

Established in 1826, the Pontoosuc Woolen Mill eventually became one of the world's largest woolen mills. This tower, constructed in the later nineteenth century, reflects the eclectic taste of the period. Note its brick arcade, corbelled cornice, polychrome slate roof, and iron cresting. Plate 24 shows the interior of the tower with its typical wooden enclosed staircase.

26 and 27. Colt Patent Fire Arms Manufactory, Hartford, Connecticut

Samuel Colt began construction of both his factory and tenements to house his workers in the mid-1850s. Long a landmark on the Hartford skyline, the bright blue, Moorish dome of the East Armory building is studded with stars and crowned with a gilded globe surmounted with the emblem of the firm, a rearing colt. This exotic symbol is clearly visible from the workers' tenements nearby (plate 26).

feet long by thirty feet wide. It had a pitched roof with a small cupola or belfry at one end, which housed a bell that regulated the hours of work.

As was common American building practice at the time, this building was constructed entirely of wood. Its heavy timber frame was covered by vertical wood siding. With the exception of a single row of wooden piers, or posts, running down the center of the building to help support the weight of the spinning machines, its floors were open from one end to the other. The machines on each of these floors were powered by long, rotating wooden shafts that ran horizontally down the entire length of the building (plate 13), which were in turn connected by geared vertical shafts to the waterwheel. Each floor was about twelve feet high to allow adequate space for the shafts and belts that powered the machinery. The work areas around the machines were illuminated by windows set into the long walls of the mill building at regular intervals.

To better light the attic of the building, a row of dormer windows called trapdoor or eyebrow monitors was cut into each side of the roof during an early-nineteenth-century remodeling (plate 11). It is likely that this motif, as well as the closely related clerestory lighting system employed in a number of other early-nineteenth-century New England mill buildings (plate 16), was based upon late-eighteenth-century English precedents. Both of these roof systems came to characterize the small American textile factory before the Civil War (plates 12, 15, and 16).

Though some early mills (plate 15) were constructed entirely of wood, more and more factories after 1800 were erected with exterior walls of either stone or brick, in response to the ever-present danger of fire. Fires were, of course, all too frequent in the textile mill. Sparks from the over-heated machinery were particularly dangerous: landing in the oil-soaked cotton scraps and waste that accumulated around the equipment, they would ignite small blazes that spread rapidly. Thus, as the century progressed, stone or brick became the preferred material for exterior walls, with red brick eventually becoming the most popular, especially for larger factory complexes. The original 1846–47 portion of Cheshire Mill No. 1, in Harrisville, for example, has walls of granite, while its 1859–60 addition is of brick (plate 56), as are all of the larger factories in such mill towns as Lowell, Lawrence, or Manchester (plates 30, 36, and 71).

The interior structure in almost all of these buildings, however, continued to be built of wood until the end of the nineteenth century. Wood was not only abundant and cheap in New England, but was sufficiently resilient to support the long rows of textile machines that spread out along each floor. It was, of course, flammable. In an effort to contain fires, a new type of wood framing, which was initially developed in England in the mid-1820s, was commonly adopted in New England mill construction during the late 1820s and thirties.[5] This system, in which the major piers and beams were increased in size and reduced in number, eventually became known as "slow-burning construction" (plate 28) To further retard the spread of fire, smaller floor joists were eliminated

28. Baltic Cotton Mill, Baltic, Connecticut

The Baltic Mills were begun by William Sprague and his sons in 1856. The entire complex is constructed of stone with an interior framing of wood. This interior is an example of slow-burning construction.

and four-inch-thick floors consisting of two layers of planking laid at right angles to one another were placed directly on top of the timber beams. This method of construction created fewer of the air pockets and hollows that trapped heat and flames, while the massive framing timbers were more likely to char on the surface than burn through quickly, allowing workers extra time to localize and extinguish fires before they spread to entire buildings.

The stair tower became a common feature in factory construction in the United States during the second decade of the nineteenth century. Many towers had an exterior door on each floor, so that raw and finished materials could be raised and lowered between floors by means of hoists and pulleys (plate 59). Besides freeing the interior spaces for manufacturing, the staircase and hoist area could be closed off from the rest of the building with heavy doors in the event of a fire, thus helping to prevent its rapid spread from one floor to another. Bathrooms were often housed in these towers.

Along with the cupola, the utilitarian—yet highly visible—tower typically received a more decorative treatment than other parts of the factory. Especially after the Civil War, the stairway and cupola tended to be combined into a single prominent tower, elaborately ornamented in any one of a wide variety of historic styles. Bell and clock towers (plates 17–22, 24, 25, 27, and 82) not only reflect the wildly eclectic tastes of the later nineteenth century, but mark the mill as the economic heart of the community. With their strong civic and ecclesiatical associations, first the cupola, and then the factory tower, became symbols of both capitalist enterprise and the conservative paternalism of the new industrialists who were reordering American urban life during this period.

Once the small textile mill took shape, it remained remarkably resistant to change for nearly a century. Small nineteenth-century industrial plants similar to the Cheshire Mill can be found scattered throughout New England, as well as in the Midwest and Middle Atlantic states. With the exception of an occasional Lombard tower (plate 20) or Moorish dome (plate 27), even the endless vacillations of architectural style that characterized the Victorian era left scarcely a mark on these buildings. In this sense they remained as stolid and conservative in character as the American industrialists who commissioned them.

As industrial processes became more complex and companies expanded, so did the average American factory. By the later years of the nineteenth century, factories of up to seven stories stretched for hundreds of yards along the banks of New England's major rivers (plates 30, 36 and 66). Limitations in size were posed only by the need for light and the engineer's ability to convey adequate power from the headrace to the machinery. Consequently, the typical factory remained narrow in profile, so that the machinery on each floor could be powered by the single shaft running down its length. Windows in each exterior bay were made as large as possible until the wall dissolved into a thin skeletal system of brick piers with inset horizontal spandrels (plate 5).

29. Continental Mill, Lewiston, Maine

The Continental Mill is just one of half a dozen large textile mill complexes that line the banks of the Androscoggin River in Lewiston, Maine. In the foreground of this photograph can be seen a portion of the impressive canal and race system that was constructed during the nineteenth century to supply power to these factories. Also visible to the left is one of the many surviving wooden bridges that once carried the mill operatives from their tenements to their work. The Continental Mill itself was constructed in 1872 and is marked by a prominent octagonal corner tower with a convex Mansard roof.

30–32. Textile Mills, Lowell, Massachusetts

By the mid-1830s, some ten different companies, including the Appleton, Boott, and Massachusetts Mills pictured here, were operating in Lowell with nearly six thousand employees. The Boott Mill (plate 30), incorporated in 1835, is a typical example of the Lowell mills. Pictured in plate 32 is a magnificent spiral staircase in one of the towers of the Massachusetts Cotton Mill, which was likewise built in the 1830s. It serves as an excellent example of the high level of craftsmanship that can be found in industrial buildings of this period and stands as a testament to the skill of the traditional New England carpenter. Board and batten wood construction was also used for the Appleton Mill bridge in plate 31.

33

33–38. Amoskeag Mills, Manchester, New Hampshire

33–38. Amoskeag Mills, Manchester, New Hampshire

The first textile mill in what, in 1810, was to become Manchester, New Hampshire, was constructed by Benjamin Prichard on the Merrimack River near the Amoskeag Falls in 1805. Sixteen years later the Boston Associates incorporated the Amoskeag Manufacturing Company with the intention of developing an industrial city on the Lowell model at this site, and they soon began erecting mills such as those seen in plate 36. Plate 33 illustrates the triangular stone foundation of one of these mills.

By the early twentieth century, the Amoskeag Mill Company, was said to be the largest textile manufacturing complex in the world. Many of its employees were housed in "corporation boarding houses," of the type seen in plates 37 and 38, which the company began erecting in the 1840s. Their lives were regulated by the factory bell (plate 34), which was housed in one of the stair towers. These towers were variously ornamented: note the austere triangular form of the copper-sheathed hipped roof of the tower photographed in plate 35, which has taken on the fine patina of age.

As the need for greater floor space increased, the pitched roof with monitor lights began to give way after mid-century to the fashionable Mansard roof (plates 21 and 29) or the more utilitarian flat roof (plates 5 and 79). Either of these configurations allowed for more usable space in the attic story and conformed more closely to the rectilinear form of the underlying slow-burning mill construction, which itself continued to be used until the end of the nineteenth century. It was the flat roof, however, that was eventually destined to become the more characteristic of the two roof forms in American industrial design during the later nineteenth and twentieth centuries.[6]

Attempts to replace the traditional wood framing with "fireproof" iron construction met with minimal success. Cast-iron columns were used occasionally (plates 61 and 75), but cast- and wrought-iron columns and beams tended to buckle and deform when exposed to the intense heat of a factory fire, leading to the rapid collapse of entire buildings. Only late in the century was it discovered that metal construction could be protected from heat with terra-cotta and, later, asbestos sheathing. By this time, however, Ernest L. Ransome was already beginning to promote his reinforced-concrete construction, a system which he, and men like C.A.P. Turner in Minneapolis or Julius and Albert Kahn in Detroit, would perfect in their "daylight" factories of the first decades of the twentieth century; buildings that ultimately replaced the traditional nineteenth-century mill (plate 39).[7]

Likewise, even though steam engines had begun to be used widely throughout the United States for smaller industrial applications by the end of the Civil War, water remained the most economical means of generating large quantities of power for the factory until the beginning of the twentieth century. The water turbine, which produced power more efficiently than the waterwheel, was perfected in France and began to be used widely in the United States after 1850.[8] Thus, industries continued to congregate along large rivers or near major falls, and it was not until the electric motor was perfected toward the end of the nineteenth century that the factory could be liberated from its geographic bondage to flowing water. Electric power, along with the development of the electric light bulb, burst the limits previously imposed on plant design. When each machine had its own source of power it no longer had to be located along the line of a single power shaft, and manufacturing could be decentralized in more economical complexes of single-story buildings that could be illuminated with electric light and therefore enclose much larger areas. These factories, too, could be located anywhere in the country.

The Growth of the Modern Industrial Community

Along with the growth of the textile companies and their factories in New England in the nineteenth century came a concomitant need to provide housing and services for the workers. At

35

least until the second decade of the nineteenth century in the main industrial centers, and in many areas until much later, the yarn produced in the mills was still woven by hand. Looms for this process were commonly located nearby in small cottages, where they were often operated by the wives and children of the men who ran and repaired the heavier spinning machinery in the mills. These cottages as well as larger boarding houses were erected more often than not by the mill owner and rented to the workers in an effort to attract a reliable and relatively stable supply of labor to the vicinity of the mill (plates 60 and 72). Most factory owners also operated company stores, which sold merchandise to the mill operatives. This paternalistic arrangement, known as the Rhode Island system after the place of its origin, allowed the factory owner or manager to closely supervise his work force and maintain order in the community. Although the adoption of the power loom during the second decade of the nineteenth century inevitably led to an expansion of operations within the factory itself, the Rhode Island system continued to serve as a model throughout the century for hundreds of small factory villages in Rhode Island and neighboring areas of Connecticut and Massachusetts.[9]

To us, removed as we are from the gritty reality of the past, these small mill villages often appear deceptively picturesque. It is all too easy to forget that their ultimate purpose was to produce textiles in the most efficient and economical manner possible, and that to this end, a twelve- or thirteen-hour work day was mandatory for all employees. Children, if too young to tend the machines themselves, were required to sit under the looms and spinning frames picking lint off of the yarn or retying the ends of broken threads. Because it was necessary to maintain a high level of humidity when spinning cotton, factory windows were often nailed shut. Consequently, the air inside of the mill was typically polluted with high levels of cotton lint and dust and the noise from the crude machinery deafening. Conditions in these communities marked a significant shift from the traditional life of the pre-industrial agricultural village.

An even more radical step away from this arcadian past was taken in 1813, when a group of Boston merchants, led by Frances Cabot Lowell, formed the Boston Manufacturing Company in Waltham, Massachusetts.[10] Lowell himself had traveled to Britain in 1811 to inspect English textile machinery. Upon his return, and with the help of American mechanics, he had been able to synthesize the latest English and American technology into a system that promised to integrate in a single factory all phases of cotton textile manufacturing, from the processing and spinning of raw cotton to the power weaving of the cloth itself. The combined capital of the corporation made an enterprise of this magnitude possible.

In order to house this operation, Lowell and his associates had two large red-brick factory buildings constructed end to end along the Charles River at Waltham between 1814 and 1816. These mills were each four stories in height with spacious attics illuminated by clerestory monitors. A single headrace, which led from a damned-up pond on the Charles, supplied power to both buildings. During this same period the Boston Manufacturing Company also erected boarding houses for its factory workers. The integration of all of the stages of textile production, from raw cotton to finished cloth, in a single, planned industrial facility, as well as the closely associated construction of large-scale tenement housing for the workers, marked a new stage in the evolution of the modern factory and factory town. This new "Waltham system" also greatly increased the productivity, as well as the potential profitability, of the American textile industry.

Although Lowell died in 1817, two of his associates, Nathan Appleton and P. T. Jackson, in partnership with Kirk Boott, chartered a second corporation, the Merrimack Company, in 1822.[11] This enterprise, again using the Waltham system, was intended to produce textiles on an even larger scale at a site on the Merrimack River near Chelmsford, Massachusetts. Here they laid out a fully planned factory town, a community which, four years later, would be named Lowell in honor of the founder of the system upon which it was based (plates 30–32). Within a decade this small village was transformed into the industrial city described by the Frenchman Michael Chevalier, when he visited it in June of 1834. "The town of Lowell," he wrote in his official report on this visit,

dates its origin eleven years ago, and it now contains fifteen thousand inhabitants, inclusive of the suburb of Belvedere. Twelve years ago it was a barren waste, in which the silence was interrupted only by the murmur of the little river of Concord, and the noisy dashings of the clear waters of the Merrimac [sic], against the granite blocks that suddenly obstruct their course. At present, it is a pile of huge factories, each five, six, or seven stories high, and capped with a little white belfry, which strongly contrasts with the red masonry of the building, and is distinctly projected on the dark hills in the horizon. By the side of these larger structures rise numerous little houses, painted white, with green blinds, very neat, very snug, very nicely carpeted, and with a few small trees around them, or brick houses in the English style, that is to say, simple, but tasteful without and comfortable within; on one side, fancy-goods shops and milliners' rooms without number, for the women are the majority in Lowell, and vast hotels in the American Style, very much like barracks (the only barracks in Lowell); on another, canals, waterwheels, waterfalls, bridges, banks, schools, and libraries. . . . Everywhere is heard the noise of hammers, of spindles, of bells calling the hands to their work, or dismissing them from their tasks, of coaches and six arriving and starting off, of the blowing of rocks to make a mill-race or to level a road; it is the peaceful hum of an industrious population, whose movements are regulated like clockwork; a population not native to the town, and one half of which at least will die elsewhere, after having aided in founding three or four other towns; for the full-blooded American has this in common with the Tartar, that he is encamped, not established, on the soil he treads upon.[12]

These "other towns" would include such major textile centers as Manchester, New Hampshire, or Lawrence, Massachusetts, both of which were modeled after Lowell and also located on

38

the banks of the Merrimack River (plates 33–38 and 71). All of these industrial centers were planned on an unprecedented scale. The Merrimack Company in Lowell, for example, comprised five uniform red-brick mill buildings, each four to five stories in height. Power was distributed to these factories and to the other textile companies that were soon operating in the city via a complex network of canals and races, which led along the south side of the river from a basin that had been formed upstream above the Pawtucket Falls. At the Merrimack Company alone, the water that traveled through this system turned eight great wheels, each of which measured some thirty feet in diameter.

By 1833, ten different companies, often with interlocking directorates, employing nearly six thousand souls, were producing textile products in Lowell. The majority of these workers were female; young women drawn from New England farms, many of which by the third decade of the century were in a state of decline, their soil depleted and overworked. Newly arriving immigrants, moreover, were willing to undertake domestic service on small farms for lower wages than the native-born girls, who traditionally took such positions to earn their dowries.[13] Consequently, many young New England farm women were forced to seek employment in the rapidly expanding industrial communities, which themselves were developing a voracious appetite for cheap labor. "Moderate farmers instead of seeing, as *formerly,* their daughters securely and honorably employed in a neighbor's service, watched over, and cared for, as children and friends," lamented one Vermont farmer in 1847,

now see them quitting home, friends, and paternal guardianship, to throng to the factories of Manchester, Lowell and Andover, where they are shut up for thirteen hours a day, where they are allowed but ten minutes to eat their dinners, and are forced to sleep in brick pens rather than comfortable rooms, exposed . . . to the thousand temptations of a crowded city; a promiscuous population and ill-chosen associates, and without home, friends or counselors, wearing life to decay, and weaving themselves shrouds whilst earning a gown.[14]

The average weekly wage for the Lowell girls was about $2.50, which they earned for working twelve to thirteen hours a day, six days a week. When not at work in the mills, they lived carefully supervised lives in nearby boarding houses, especially constructed by the companies in neat rectilinear rows next to the factories. For room and board, $1.25 a week was deducted from the girls' wages. Similar conditions existed in many of the other New England textile communities that were the products of this era: cities such as Lawrence, New Bedford, and Fall River, Massachusetts; Manchester, Dover, Nashua, and Laconia, New Hampshire; Willimantic and Hartford, Connecticut; or Burlington, Vermont.

39. Seth Thomas Clock Company, Thomaston, Connecticut

Although Seth Thomas, Sr., began to assemble clocks in what was to become the town of Thomaston as early as 1813, the Seth Thomas Clock Company was not incorporated until 1853. After this date its facilities grew rapidly, covering some twenty acres of floor space by 1880. Visible in this photograph are some of the modest workers' houses which compose the town and one of the Seth Thomas Clock Company buildings, an early-twentieth-century "daylight" factory of reinforced-concrete construction. This type of construction was destined, during the first decades of this century, to replace the traditional mill construction pioneered in the textile mills of the previous century.

Typical of the boarding houses erected by the large mill companies in the 1830s and forties are the long blocks of red-brick tenements in Manchester, New Hampshire (plate 37). Later these same structures would house the successive waves of immigrants destined to replace farm girls in the mills: the Irish, Germans, Italians, Eastern Europeans, Blacks, and Hispanics, or, like the Kerouacs, French Canadians.[15]

By the end of the nineteenth century, New England mills produced about half of all the woolen goods, and four-fifths of the cotton fabrics manufactured in the United States. Textile complexes were expanded to vast proportions. The largest of them, the Amoskeag Mill Company in Manchester, begun by the Boston Associates in 1838, eventually employed as many as seventeen thousand people who were said to produce fabric at a rate of a mile a minute on twenty-four thousand looms (plates 33–38).[16] By 1915 its facilities encompassed some sixty acres of floor space and stretched a full mile along both banks of the Merrimack River. Numerous other textile plants, in Fall River, Lowell, Lawrence, or Willimantic, were almost comparable in scale.

These industries, because of their size and organization, were ultimately the decisive catalyst for a shift from an economy dependent upon traditional agriculture to one based upon manufacturing processes in nineteenth-century New England. The industrial revolution, beginning with the introduction of the Arkwright system, marked a cataclysmic break with the past that would prove as significant in shaping the future course and form of the United States as the political revolt that had preceeded it by a mere decade and a half. It would also create what the British architectural historian Reyner Banham has called "one of the most successful vernacular building types in the recent history of architecture," the American factory building of the nineteenth century.[17] This building, along with the new villages and cities that grew up around it, shaped the New England countryside as we know it today.

Notes

1. For a thorough description of this era see John R. Stilgoe, *Common Landscape of America, 1580–1845.*

2. Richard M. Candee, "New Towns of the Early New England Textile Industry," pp. 31–34.

3. For a general introduction to the early development of textile machinery and mills see John Winter, *Industrial Architecture, A Survey of Factory Building.*

4. For the evolution and significance of the Old Slater Mill see William H. Pierson, Jr., *American Buildings and Their Architects: Technology and the Picturesque, The Corporate and Early Gothic Style,* pp. 22–49.

5. Candee, "New Towns of the Early New England Textile Industry," p. 45; and Pierson, *American Buildings and Their Architects,* p. 49.

6. Reyner Banham, *Concrete Atlantis: U.S. Industrial Building and European Modern Architecture 1900–1925,* pp. 38–39.

7. Ibid., pp. 23–107; and Moritz Kahn, *The Design and Construction of Industrial Buildings.*

8. Winter, *Industrial Architecture,* p. 44.

9. Candee, "New Towns of the Early New England Textile Industry," pp. 37–38.

10. Ibid., p. 38; and Pierson, *American Buildings and Their Architects,* pp. 59–63.

11. Ibid., pp. 59–63. See also John Coolidge, *Mill and Mansion, a Study of Architecture and Society in Lowell, Massachusetts, 1820–1865.*

12. Michael Chevalier, *Society, Manners and Politics in the United States being a series of letters on North America.*

13. See, for example, Thomas Dublin, *Women at Work: The Transformation of Work and Community in Lowell, Massachusetts, 1826–1860.*

14. John Orvis, "Trip to Vermont," pp. 50–52.

15. Donald Cole, *Immigrant City: Lawrence, 1845–1921.*

16. Tamara K. Hareven and Randolph Langenbach, *Amoskeag: Life and Work in an American Factory-City.*

17. Banham, *Concrete Atlantis,* p. 41.

40 and 41. Town Grist Mill, Hampton, New Hampshire

Although erected in 1832, this gristmill, like the Little River Mill in East Lebanon, Maine (plate 3), is typical of the scale of the majority of American industrial buildings constructed prior to the introduction of textile spinning and weaving machinery. Millstones, worn down from grinding grain into flour, are used as steps leading into the mill (plate 41).

42 and 43. Old Schwamb Mill, Arlington, Massachusetts

The Schwamb family began producing picture frames at this site in 1847, and the mill as it appears today represents a rare survival of a small nineteenth-century industrial enterprise. The main factory, dating from about 1860, is now operated as a museum. It still possesses an array of belt- and pulley-driven lathes and other wood-working tools, as well as a wood-drying kiln. An old millstone serves as a front step to the office (plate 43)

44. Lowell Boat Company, Amesbury, Massachusetts

The heavy beams and joists characteristic of a traditional wood-framed building can be seen in this view of the Lowell Boat Company. A similar refinement of wood-building technology is also applied to the construction of the small skiffs and dories that have been produced in this building since the end of the eighteenth century.

45. Brownell Twine Mill, Moodus, Connecticut

This mid-nineteenth-century mill was erected by the Brownell family to spin cotton twine for fishing nets. During the nineteenth and first half of the twentieth centuries, this small Connecticut River Valley town was home to a thriving twine-making industry. As late as 1930, it still possessed a dozen such factories. Today, only two remain.

46. Contoocook Mill, Hillsboro, New Hampshire

On a precipitous site on the south bank of the Contoocook River, just upstream from the Marcy Mill (plate 15), John Butler Smith constructed the first two floors of this mill in 1865 for the manufacture of woolen goods. As Smith's enterprise grew, the building was expanded to its present configuration and became the center of a complex that included several other factory structures. In 1882 Smith Mills was incorporated as the Contoocook Mills Corporation.

47. Turner Machine Company, Danbury, Connecticut

Erected during the last quarter of the nineteenth century, this two-story, wood-frame factory building formed part of the Turner Machine Company complex on Maple Street in Danbury. The company produced hat-making machinery, much of which was employed locally by Danbury hat makers during the late nineteenth and first half of the twentieth centuries. The building has been destroyed since this photograph was taken.

48. Herreshoff Manufacturing Company, Bristol, Rhode Island

The Herreshoff Manufacturing Company purchased the Burnside rifle factory in the 1870s to expand its production of steam launches and yachts, and continued to add onto this complex well into the twentieth century. This wood-frame factory building encloses a space three stories high.

49. Estey Organ Works, Brattleboro, Vermont

The Estey Organ Company occupied a complex of half a dozen wood-frame factories dating from the 1870s. The buildings have gray slate shingle siding and, like the American Woolen Mill in Skowhegan, Maine (plate 50), multi-pane sash windows.

50. American Woolen Factory, Skowhegan, Maine

This late-nineteenth-century woolen mill is now the home of New Balance Athletic Shoes. In spite of its shingle siding, it possesses the prominent stair and freight tower and maximum fenestration characteristic of the American factory of this period.

51 and 52. Pejepscot (Topsham) Paper Mill, Topsham, Maine

The Topsham Paper Company constructed the fine, three-and-a-half story brick mill in plate 51 at Brunswick Falls on the Androscoggin River in 1868. In 1874, the mill was purchased by the Bowdoin Paper Company, which, along with such other Maine enterprises as S. D. Warren (plate 73), pioneered the use of wood pulp in the manufacture of paper. It is the oldest remaining wood-pulp paper mill in Maine.

53 and 54. The Hockanum Mill Company, Rockville, Connecticut

The Hockanum Mill is situated directly upriver from the Saxony Mill (plate 55) and not far from the Florence Mill (plate 82) in Rockville. The main portion of this factory, a two-and-a-half-story wood-frame building set on a brick basement, was built in the 1850s. In 1880, a new office with a prominent Mansard roof was erected to the east of this structure. A small addition also was added to the west end of the main mill during the 1870s.

55. Saxony Mill, Rockville, Connecticut

The Saxony Mill was just one of numerous textile factories located along the Hockanum River during the nineteenth century (see plates 53 and 82). Erected in 1836, the Saxony Mill is constructed entirely of wood and has a tall central stair tower, part of which can be seen to the far right of this view. The attic is lit with a series of dormer windows with triangular gables, set symmetrically to either side of the tower.

56. Cheshire Mill No. 1, Harrisville, New Hampshire

The first factory erected in Harrisville by Bethuel Harris and his son Cyrus in 1822 was devoted to the manufacture of woolen textiles. A second mill, of brick, was built in 1832, and Cheshire Mill No. 1, the only building in Harrisville of granite masonry construction, in the following decade. Its stone construction and clerestory monitor appear to have been derived from southern New England textile factories of several decades earlier. The village of Harrisville, itself, with its remarkably preserved complex of factories, boarding houses, and churches, represents a rare survival of a mid-nineteenth-century American industrial community.

57. Woonsocket Company, Mill No. 4, Woonsocket, Rhode Island

Erected in 1859 along the Blackstone River in the Bernon area of Woonsocket, this factory, which has recently been restored, was the last building to be completed in a complex that began with one mill belonging to the Russell Manufacturing Company in 1827. During the following decade, the operation was purchased by the Woonsocket Company, which constructed three more mills. Although all four mill buildings had walls of random-coursed ashlar, only this last one incorporated a prominent row of dormers with Greek Revival pediments into its roof.

58. Willimantic Linen Factory, Willimantic, Connecticut

The Willimantic Linen Factory was organized in 1854 by Austin Durham. Its neoclassically styled mill, erected during the Civil War, was the first in the United States to employ a steam-heated and moisturized atmosphere to facilitate the production of fine linen thread. In 1898, the company's name was changed to the Willimantic Thread Company.

59–61. Hope Mill and Workers Houses, Hope, Rhode Island

The Hope Mill was completed by the Hope Cotton Manufacturing Company in 1844 and enlarged in the 1870s, when the company also constructed the small, Mansard-roofed, double houses for its workers that can be seen in the foreground of plate 60. Note the wood picket gates that enclose the freight doors at each level of the tower and the small pulleys, which still hang from the ridge of the tower roof, used to haul material to these doors. The interior of the Hope Mill (plate 61) exhibits a modified slow-burning construction, with cast-iron columns replacing the more common wooden piers.

62. Pokanoket Mill, Bristol, Rhode Island

Seen here is the loading dock of the original stone factory of the Pokanoket textile mill, erected in 1839 by the Richmond Manufacturing Company. At each story above the dock are freight doors with wood picket gates, through which raw and manufactured materials could be hoisted directly to the floors of the factory.

63. Robinson and Company Fur Shop, Danbury, Connecticut

Peter Robinson, a Canadian-born furrier, had this mill erected on Oil Mill Road in 1882 to house a fur-cutting operation. The gambrel roof was added after a fire destroyed the upper floor in 1896. The factory was placed on the National Register of Historic Places in 1982, and has since been converted into luxury apartments.

64. Workers' Housing, Adams, Massachusetts

These brick row houses were constructed during the second half of the nineteenth century to house the families that worked in Adams's many textile mills. With their segmentally arched windows and corbelled brick cornices, these structures bore few external differences from the factories in which their occupants labored.

65. Austin Block, New Castle, New Hampshire

The Austin Block was erected in 1845 as a tenement for shipyard workmen in New Castle. Constructed of brick with a granite water table and lintels, this boarding house bears a close resemblance to the simple Neoclassical tenements erected in the 1830s and forties in mill towns such as Lowell or Manchester.

66–70. Saco and Biddeford, Maine

The textile mills in Biddeford and Saco were constructed on either side of the Saco River where it drops fifty-five feet to the Atlantic Ocean. Both cities are currently in the midst of considerable redevelopment as their economies shift away from the once prosperous textile industry. While companies such as West Point Pepperell (plate 67) still operate plants in Biddeford, many of the mills on Saco Island, which can be seen to the right in plate 66, have recently begun to undergo renovation as apartments, retail stores, and offices. The small factory on Water Street in Saco, pictured in plate 68, in fact, has already been heavily altered—so as to be hardly recognizable—and turned into luxury apartments since this photograph was taken. And working-class institutions, such as the Pepperell Social and Athletic Club (foreground of plate 70), which was sponsored by the company for its workers, or the bar whose window reflects a view of the Biddeford Textile Company (plate 69), are quickly becoming things of the past.

67

69

68

71. Lower Pacific Mills, Lawrence, Massachusetts

The Lower Pacific Mills, which were part of the Pacific Mills complex begun in 1852, were themselves erected in 1868. They were constructed parallel to one of two canals that ran along the banks of the Merrimack River. Water was fed to these canals by means of a 900-foot-long stone dam that traversed the river, forming a 28-foot head of water capable of producing 12,000 horsepower. Visible in this photograph are walkways or bridges that connected the various plants. By the 1920s, the Pacific Mills had grown to be one of the largest wool and cotton manufacturing complexes in the country, encompassing some 27 brick buildings, with 135 acres of floor space.

72 and 73. Cumberland Mills and Workers Houses of the S. D. Warren Company, Westbrook, Maine

The S. D. Warren Company was a nineteenth-century pioneer in the use of wood pulp, as opposed to rag pulp, for the making of paper. Maine, in particular, with its abundance of trees and plentiful water supply, became a center of paper production after this development. The modest Queen Anne cottages seen in plate 72 were erected by the company on Brown Street in Westbrook in 1881 to house its workers. They seem to have been designed by the prominent Portland architect, John Calvin Stevens, who in 1880 had supervised the construction of a similar series of mill workers' cottages for the Forest Fibre Company in Berlin, New Hampshire. By 1883, S. D. Warren owned one hundred and fifty such homes, which were rented to its employees for between $75.00 and $300.00 a year.

74 and 75. Cocheco Manufacturing Company,
Dover, New Hampshire

*This factory complex, constructed in 1880–81, spans
the Cocheco River on a steel-reinforced brick arch. In
the foreground is the millpond, formed by damming up
the river just above the Cocheco Falls. This location
had been the site of waterpowered industries since the
first sawmill was erected here in 1642–44. The interior of this factory (plate 75) is framed with a combina-
tion of cast-iron columns and heavy wooden beams to
retard fire.*

Overleaf
76. Bourne Mill, Tiverton, Rhode Island

*Erected just outside of Fall River at the head of Cook
Pond in 1881–82, the Bourne Mill is just one of
dozens in Fall River and its immediate vicinity. Like
many of these textile factories, the Bourne Mill was
constructed of local granite and had a slightly pitched
(almost flat) roof, with a prominent central stair tower.*

78. Towle Manufacturing Company,
Newburyport, Massachusetts

*The Towle Silver Company was founded by A. F.
Towle and W. P. Jones in 1857, but it was not until
1883 that it occupied this brick factory, constructed in
1866 by the Merrimack Arms and Manufacturing
Company. Note the fine Mansard-roofed stair tower
and segmentally arched windows.*

77. Merchant's Cold Storage Warehouse,
Providence, Rhode Island

*Massive ogival arches and blind arcades of brick orna-
ment the back facade of the Merchant's Cold Storage
Warehouse, erected in the produce district of Providence in 1893. Because this structure was intended for
the cold storage of produce, only small windows punc-
tuate its walls, most of which have since been bricked
in.*

Overleaf, left:
79. Alice Mill, Woonsocket, Rhode Island

*The Alice Mill, with its two prominent Italianate stair
towers with hipped roofs, was constructed in 1889. Its
thin piers and large segmentally arched windows are
characteristic of late-nineteenth and early-twentieth-
century factory construction. The original sash windows have been replaced with hinged glass panels.*

Overleaf, right:
80. Luther Mill, Fall River, Massachusetts

*The Luther Textile Mill was originally erected as one
of two Robeson Mills in 1870–71. It became the
Luther Mill in 1903 when it was taken over by the
Luther Manufacturing Company, incorporated that
same year. Constructed of brick, with segmentally
arched lintels set between vertical piers, this mill dis-
plays a fine octagonal stair tower ornamented in its
upper stories with blind arcades.*

81. Scovill Manufacturing Company, Waterbury, Connecticut

The Scovill Manufacturing Company is only one of many brass mills that have operated in Waterbury since the early part of the nineteenth century. Although not incorporated until 1850, the company had been growing rapidly since it began to manufacture daguerreotype plates and other photographic supplies in 1842. By 1895, it employed some sixteen hundred workers in what was said to be the largest brass works in the country. The parts of the factory pictured in this photograph date for the most part from the last quarter of the nineteenth century. In the foreground can be seen the sawtooth roof and exhaust chimneys of the smelters.

82. Florence Mill, Rockville, Connecticut

In 1881, this textile mill was purchased by White, Corbin and Company to be used for the manufacture of envelopes. The upper story of the mill and tower were reconstructed after a fire in 1882, and the original ornate design of 1864 was retained. This included a gambrel roof with dormers and ocular end windows to light the attic of the factory. The tower has a richly corbelled cornice set over broad arches and smaller ocular windows and finely chamfered corners on its upper stories, giving it an especially elegant appearance. Originally a flag pole graced the apex of its gently curved and hipped roof.

83. South Berwick Shoe Company, South Berwick, Maine

Like many other industries, the shoe-manufacturing business adopted the brick and wood-framed mill construction that had been pioneered by the textile companies of Rhode Island and Massachusetts. This small factory in South Berwick, like many others of its type in New England, is now unoccupied.

84. Wholesale Warehouses, Concord, New Hampshire

Constructed during the last quarter of the nineteenth century on Bridge Street between Concord's commercial district and the railroad yards, these warehouses were home to wholesale grocers, metalsmiths, and furniture and plumbing distributors. The small brick building to the left, for example, for many decades housed the offices and warehouse of Dickerman, Leavitt and Company, Wholesale Grocers. The tall smokestack in the background was built in the twentieth century by the Concord Steam Company, which also occupied a portion of this site for a number of years.

85. Davol Manufacturing Company, Providence, Rhode Island

The Davol Manufacturing Company, originally the Perkins Manufacturing Company and, after 1882, the Davol Rubber Company, was organized by Joseph Davol and Emery Perkins during the last quarter of the nineteenth century to produce experimental rubber products. The two buildings pictured here are part of a larger complex that grew up to house this enterprise, and they seem particularly illustrative of the evolution of the American factory. The structure on the right, which was completed in 1884, is brick with heavy timber framing in the tradition of earlier mill construction, while its neighbor to the left, erected in 1913, possesses a steel frame and much larger windows. In 1960 it received a glass and steel fourth floor, and since 1980 the entire complex has been converted into a mixed-use commercial development, with glass-enclosed atrium courtyards and a pseudo-historic cornice and tower.

86. Heating Plant for the Rhode Island State House, Providence, Rhode Island

In the foreground of this view of the Rhode Island State House, designed by the prominent New York architectural firm of McKim, Mead and White, can be seen the small heating plant that produced steam to heat the Capitol building. The State House complex was begun in 1895 and dedicated in 1904.

87 and 88. American Brass Company Offices,
Waterbury, Connecticut

*The American Brass Company came into existence in
1899 when the Waterbury and Coe brass companies
merged with Ansonia Brass and Copper, forming the
largest producer of brass products in the world. It was
soon after this that it erected a corporate office building
in downtown Waterbury to mark the formation of this
new firm. Of brick, with Classical terra-cotta orna-
mentation, its long, gracefully curving facade is ac-
cented with an impressive brass entryway, which cele-
brates the company's products.*

Overleaf
89. Elliot Rose Company Greenhouses,
Madbury, New Hampshire

*During the first quarter of this century, the Elliot Rose
Company, which was started in 1902, was the largest
producer of roses in the East and one of the largest such
operations in the country. Its hundreds of yards of
greenhouses were constructed between 1902 and about
1920. They are heated with steam produced in the
heating plant visible in the background of this
photograph.*

90. Smokestack, Mount Vernon, Maine

This lone smokestack is all that remains to remind us of a factory or mill that once stood alongside this dam in Maine. Like many other early industrial sites in New England, it has gained with the passing of time a certain romantic, if somewhat melancholic, patina. For better or worse, it has merged into the familiar New England landscape.

Bibliography

Armstrong, John Borden. *Factory Under the Elms: A History of Harrisville, N.H. 1774–1969*. Cambridge, Massachusetts: The MIT Press, 1969.

Bagnell, William R. *The Textile Industries of the United States*. Cambridge, Massachusetts: Riverside Press, 1893.

Banham, Reyner. *Concrete Atlantis: U.S. Industrial Building and European Modern Architecture 1900–1925*. Cambridge, Massachusetts: The MIT Press, 1986.

Brecher, Jeremy, Jerry Lombardi, and Jan Stackhouse, editors and compilers. *Brass Valley: The Story of Working Peoples' Lives and Struggles in an American Industrial Region*. Philadelphia: Temple University Press, 1982.

Candee, Richard M. "New Towns of the Early New England Textile Industry," in *Perspectives in Vernacular Architecture,* ed. by Camille Wells. Annapolis, Maryland: The Vernacular Architecture Forum, 1982.

———. "The Old Schwamb Picture Frame Mill: The Preservation of a Small 19th Century Local Industry," *Pioneer America* 4 (January 1972): 1–7.

Chevalier, Michael. *Society, Manners and Politics in the United States being a series of letters on North America*. Boston: Weeks, Jordan and Company, 1839.

Clark, Victor S. *History of Manufactures in the United States*. 3 vols. Washington, D.C.: Carnegie Foundation, 1929.

Cochran, Thomas C., and William Miller. *The Age of Enterprise*. New York: Macmillan, 1942.

Cole, Donald. *Immigrant City: Lawrence, 1845–1921*. Cambridge, Massachusetts: Harvard University Press, 1963.

Coleman, Peter J. *The Transformation of Rhode Island, 1790–1860*. Providence, Rhode Island: Brown University Press, 1969.

Coolidge, John. *Mill and Mansion, a Study of Architecture and Society in Lowell, Massachusetts, 1820–1865*. New York: Columbia University Press, 1942.

Dublin, Thomas. *Women at Work: The Transformation of Work and Community in Lowell, Massachusetts, 1826–1860*. New York: Columbia University Press, 1979.

Eno, Arthur L., Jr., ed. *Cotton Was King: A History of Lowell, Massachusetts*. Lowell: Lowell Historical Society, 1976.

Hareven, Tamara K., and Randolph Langenbach. *Amoskeag: Life and Work in an American Factory-City*. New York: Pantheon Books, 1978.

Hitchcock, Henry Russell. *Rhode Island Architecture*. Cambridge, Massachusetts: The MIT Press, 1968.

Josephson, Hannah. *The Golden Threads: New England's Mill Girls and Magnates*. New York, 1949.

Kahn, Moritz. *The Design and Construction of Industrial Buildings*. London Technical Journals, 1917.

Kerouac, Jack. *The Town and the City*. New York: Harvest/HBJ Edition, 1978.

Landau, Sarah Bradford, "The Colt Industrial Empire," *Antiques* (March 1976): 568–79.

LeBlanc, R. G. *Location of Manufacturing in New England in the Nineteenth Century*. Hanover, New Hampshire: Geography Publications at Dartmouth, 1969.

Leyland, Herbert T. "Early Years of the Hope Cotton Manufacturing Company," *Rhode Island History* 25 (January 1966): 25–32.

Malone, Patrick M. *The Lowell Canal System*. Lowell, Massachusetts: The Lowell Museum, 1976.

Marx, Leo. *The Machine in the Garden: Technology and the Pastoral Ideal in America*. New York: Oxford University Press, 1969.

Orvis, John [Wendall]. "Trip to Vermont," *The Harbinger* 5 (1847): 50–52.

Pierson, William H., Jr. *American Buildings and Their Architects: Technology and the Picturesque, The Corporate and Early Gothic Style*. New York: Doubleday and Company, 1978.

Sande, Theodore Anton. *Industrial Archeology: A New Look at the American Heritage*. New York: Penguin Books, 1978.

———, and Robert Vogel, eds. *The New England Textile Mill Survey—Selections from the Historic American Buildings Survey*. Washington, D.C.: National Park Service, No. 11, 1971.

Stilgoe, John R. *Common Landscape of America, 1580–1845*. New Haven and London: Yale University Press, 1982.

Tann, Jennifer. *The Development of the Factory*. London: Cornmarket Press, 1970.

Wallace, Anthony F. C. *Rockdale: Growth of an American Village in the Early Industrial Revolution*. New York: Alfred A. Knopf, 1978.

Winter, John. *Industrial Architecture, A Survey of Factory Building*. London: Studio Vista, 1970.